SWEAR WORD COLORING BOOK

CUPCAKES

Cupcakes and Flowers Mandalas Designs

VOL.1

COLOR TEST PAGE

COLOR TEST PAGE

Fuck

Piss Off

Fuck Off

MADE WITH LOVE
idiot
CUPCAKE

Douche bag

Fuck

Piece of
Shit

Gutter
Slut

Idiot

Bitch

Asshole

Bitch
Face

Asshat

Whore

Cunt

TWAT WAFFLE

Damn

Screw
You

Bitch

Slut

Go to Hell,
Bitch!

Bellend

Hot Shit

CUM
GUZZLER

Shitballs

SUGAR TITS

Dipshit
WELCOME

Bastard

Cupcakes
Sweet & Tasty
Bullshit
BEST IN TOWN
SINCE 1992

Bitch

Bitch

Twat
Waffle

Idiot

www.ingramcontent.com/pod-product-compliance
Lightning Source LLC
Chambersburg PA
CBHW081854280526
45789CB00007B/2694
* 9 7 8 1 5 4 0 3 8 6 5 7 1 *